Ripley's

Believe It or Not!®

MC
PUBLISHERS

Mason Crest Publishers

TWISTS

Written by Geoff Tibballs
Consultant Stewart Newport

Originally published by

RiPLEY
PUBLISHING

Publisher Anne Marshall

Managing Editor Rebecca Miles
Picture Researcher James Proud
Editors Lisa Regan, Rosie Alexander
Assistant Editor Amy Harrison
Proofreader Judy Barratt
Indexer Hilary Bird

Art Director Sam South
Design Rocket Design (East Anglia) Ltd
Reprographics Stephan Davis

www.masoncrest.com

ISBN 978-1-4222-1834-1 (hardcover)

ISBN 978-1-4222-2072-6 (ppk)

Series ISBN (8 titles): 978-1-4222-1827-3

10 9 8 7 6 5 4 3 2 1

For information regarding permission, write to VP Intellectual Property, Ripley Entertainment Inc., Suite 188, 7576 Kingspointe Parkway, Orlando, Florida 32819

e-mail: publishing@ripleys.com

Library of Congress Cataloging-in-Publication Data is available.

Printed in USA

PUBLISHER'S NOTE

While every effort has been made to verify the accuracy of the entries in this book, the Publishers cannot be held responsible for any errors contained in the work. They would be glad to receive any information from readers.

WARNING: Some of the stunts and activities in this book are undertaken by experts and should not be attempted by anyone without adequate training and supervision.

CONTENTS

WHAT'S INSIDE YOUR BOOK? 4

SPEED KINGS 6
FAST AND FURIOUS

ON FOUR LEGS 8
ANIMAL ATHLETES

MAKING A SPLASH 10
WET AND WILD

TRIALS OF STRENGTH 12
FEEL THE FORCE

ON COURT 14
SHOOTING HOOPS

TWISTS

SNOW AND ICE
CHILLS AND THRILLS 16

OFF THE WALL
UNUSUAL SPORTS 18

TOUCH DOWN
CATCH AND KICK 20

PEDAL POWER
PUSHING IT 22

EXTREME ACTION
NO LIMITS 24

SHOW SOME MUSCLE
BODY POWER 26

GET YOUR SKATES ON
HEELS ON WHEELS 28

GOAL CRAZY
SENSATIONAL SOCCER 30

FLYING HIGH
TAKING TO THE SKIES 32

SURF'S UP
RIDING THE WAVES 34

IN THE RUNNING
MARATHONS 36

RISKY BUSINESS
DANGEROUS SPORTS 38

HAVING A BALL
CATCHING ON 40

WACKY RACES
FUN RUNS 42

FUN AND GAMES
OLYMPIC DREAMS 44

INDEX 46

13

3

WORLD OF SPORT

So you think you know about sport? Well, prepare to learn even more! Top sports attract millions of spectators and billions of dollars, and bring together countries across the globe to play, watch, and shout about their favorite games and competitions.

Sport isn't just about big money, clubs, and players. Some sports are played and watched by just a few people, but are just as much fun. So, if you're not into ball games, this book will introduce you to tug-of-war, BMX racing, and even worm charming. There's something here for everyone...

WHAT'S INSIDE YOUR BOOK?

Do the twist

Take a look... each page is packed with sporting superstars, amazing achievements, and of course, crazy pastimes that don't get a mention in other sports books. That's what a Twists book is all about!

twist it!

Don't forget to look out for the "twist it!" column on some pages. Twist the book to read snappy sports stories from all around the world; if you're feeling super sporty then read it standing on your head!

Welsh soccer fan Steve Thatcher named his son after all the players in his favorite team, Cardiff City. It means young Sam has 12 middle names!

An annual soccer match called the Calcio takes place in Florence, Italy, between two teams of 27 players dressed in 16th-century costume. It is a rough game, and players are allowed to head butt each other, kick, and even head butt to elbow.

Important soccer matches often attract crowds of over 70,000 people, but the 1950 World Cup final between Brazil and Uruguay was watched by nearly 200,000 spectators.

Some soccer matches are decided by penalty shoot-outs, where eight kicks are often enough to get a result. At the end of a 2005 Namibian Cup tie in Africa, the penalty contest went on for an incredible 48 kicks and lasted nearly an hour!

FULL KICKS

SPEEDY SPORTS

Sport isn't all about speed—but speed certainly makes sport exciting! See what's fastest in the world of sport...

Motorbike 360 mph

Formula 1 Car 257 mph

Learn fab fast facts to go with the cool pictures.

Ripley explains some of the science and know-how behind your favorite sports.

Say what? Oh, so that's what that word means...

SURF'S UP

RIDING THE WAVES

It's not only waves that are a danger to surfers. Each year as many as 50 surfers are attacked by sharks.

84 surfers rode the same wave at the same time off the coast of Brazil in 2007.

ve you ever shed you could a wave on a fboard? Some waves huge—up to 70 feet . That's more than four s the height of an adult fe! That just makes it even more ch   fer. You can surf a   or lying down—and some   on the same wave for half an   r just do what you enjoy.

8th century —used planks of w weight polyurethane fo m. Si California, Florida   Ha bed and strong wi s cr

Ripley explains...

You catch a wave by pushing the water toward the back of the surfboard with your hands, moving you forward. As you ride on the wave the water rises beneath you and pushes you forward faster and faster. All the time gravity is trying to push you down, while buoyancy is pushing you up.

PLAIN SAILING

Windsurfers attach a sail to their surfboards. When the wind blows into the sail from behind, it makes the board go faster, sometimes up to 60 mph! Windsurfers can perform amazing stunts, jumps, and spins.

RIDING HIGH

Kite surfers use wind power to help them speed across the water and soar up to 100 feet in the air. They stand on a board and hold on to a large controllable kite. The aim is to do tricks such as jumps, spins, and even somersaults, and to see how high and long they can jump off waves.

SAY WHAT?

CATCH A WAV

This is when you launch yourself into the path of a suitable wave.

Kite surfers can go great distances when the wind is behind them. In 2006, UK kite surfer Kirsty Jones traveled 140 miles from Lanzarote in the Canary Islands to Morocco.

Donald "D.J." Dettloff has created a colorful fence from more than 700 surfboards near his home in Hawaii.

Lauren Miller's dog Auggie liked to do tricks with tennis balls. He could pick up five in his mouth at the same time!

Ripley's Believe It or Not!

Twists are all about "Believe It or Not!"— amazing facts, feats, and things that will make you go "Wow!"

Look for the Ripley "R" to find out even more than you knew before!

Motorbike Wheelie 140 mph	**Ostrich** 45 mph	**Camel** 40 mph	**Racehorse** 40 mph	**Human** (sprinter) 23 mph

SPEED KINGS

The cars reach speeds of nearly 240 mph on the straights.

Imagine flying a plane at over 2,000 mph. Or riding a motorbike at 360 mph. Or driving a speedboat at 300 mph. Wow! Ever since vehicles were invented, people have wanted them to go as fast as possible. We love speed. That's why we dream of one day racing in NASCAR or driving in a Formula-1 race. The cars there can go from 0 to 100 mph and back to 0 in under five seconds.

Three drivers (AJ Foyt, Al Unser, and Rick Mears) have won four Indy 500s.

Jamaica's Usain Bolt doesn't need an engine to go fast. He can run at amazing speeds. In 100-meter races he averages just over 23 mph but for a few strides he actually reaches 30 mph. That's the speed limit for a car in most towns!

The Indy 500 is probably the most famous motor race in the world. About 400,000 people turn up to watch—and millions more see it on TV in more than 160 countries. The 500-mile race takes place every year at the oval-shaped Indianapolis Motor Speedway in Indiana.

CRAZY CORNERING

As they go round corners, motorbike racers lean their machines at almost impossible angles of 50 degrees without falling off. The riders have their knee just a few inches off the ground to work out how much they can lean before their bike loses balance and topples over.

Fire-proof hood

HIGH SPEED FURNACE

Formula-1 drivers need to be amazingly fit. The temperature in the car reaches 122°F and drivers get very hot beneath their fire-proof overalls. They lose an average of 4½ pounds in body weight during each race. When braking and cornering, the pull on the driver's neck is so great that it feels as if their head wants to roll off their shoulders!

Flame-resistant driving suit

When the Indy 500 was first raced in 1911, the track was made up of 3.2 million bricks, earning it the nickname "The Brickyard."

MOTORHEADS

The first car race was run in France from Paris to Rouen in 1894. The average winning speed was just over 11 mph!

English farmer George Shields drives a garden shed that can do 55 mph. He once drove it all the way from one end of Britain to the other. That's over 800 miles.

C.G. Mouch of Los Angeles fitted the front end of a 75cc Honda motorcycle to the rear end of his lawn mower to create a "chopper mower" that could mow the lawn at up to 10 mph.

The 1972 Bandama Car Rally in West Africa was so tough that none of the 52 starters finished.

In 2005, Australian Matt Mingay did a motorbike wheelie at a speed of 140 mph.

FACT IT!

LIGHTNING BOLT

Jamaican runner Usain Bolt won the 100 meters at the 2008 Beijing Olympics in an incredible 9.69 seconds—despite slowing down to celebrate and having his left shoelace undone!

ON FOUR LEGS

ANIMAL ATHLETES

Racehorses are bred for speed. These thoroughbreds, as they are known, can gallop at up to 40 mph. Horse racing dates back nearly 3,000 years to the ancient Greeks who added the spectacular sport of chariot racing to the Olympics in 680 BCE. Horse racing is so popular today that in Switzerland there is even a horse race on ice, run on a frozen lake.

There are also races for animals that you might not think are built for speed, such as camels, armadillos, pigs, and sheep. Whatever the animal, there is probably a race for it somewhere in the world. We don't only race animals. We wrestle them, we ski behind them, and in parts of Asia polo is played on elephants instead of horses.

HORSE POWER

In the Palio, which takes place twice each summer, horses race at breakneck speed three times around the main square in Siena, Italy—and the riders don't even have saddles to sit on. No wonder so many fall off!

Around 60,000 people squeeze into the square to watch the colorful race.

The Palio was first raced in 1656 and has remained largely the same ever since.

A bank of mattresses is positioned to protect the horses and riders from the walls of a café at a turn known as the "corner of death."

Jockeys are usually small, but they also have to be strong, because racehorses can weigh up to 1,500 pounds.

DERBY

A derby is a type of race. The original derby, a horserace run in Epsom, England, was named after the Earl of Derby who founded the event in 1780.

JUMBO POLO

Polo is usually played on horseback, but in countries like Nepal, India, and Thailand they play it with elephants. Two people ride each elephant—one to steer the elephant, the other to hit the ball. The mallet used to strike the ball is made of bamboo and can be up to 12 feet long, depending on the height of the elephant. If a player falls off, it's a long way down!

twist it!

RACING AROUND

The Frog Derby takes place in Rayne, Louisiana, where kids dress frogs in miniature jockey uniforms! By tapping the ground behind the frogs, they encourage them to hop along the course in leaps and bounds.

At an annual round-up in Stephensville, Wisconsin, participants try to wrestle slippery, squirming pigs to the ground in thick mud.

You may have heard of greyhound racing. Well, in Oklahoma City, they have a dog race with a difference: It's only for little dachshunds and it's called the Dachshund Dash.

Back in 1937, a man in England tried to stage cheetah racing as an alternative to greyhounds. The cheetahs showed no interest in running, however, and often just stood still.

A racehorse named Camarero won 56 races in a row in Puerto Rico between 1953 and 1955.

<< PIG OLYMPICS >>

It's not only humans that have their own Olympics. There is also an Olympic Games for pigs! Miniature pigs run over hurdles, compete in swimming races, and play a version of soccer called pigball, where they chase a ball covered in fish oil with their snouts.

DESERT DERBY

In the Middle East and Australia, camel racing is a serious sport with big prize money. Top racing camels sell for up to $40,000. Camels can run as fast as 40 mph in short sprints and can maintain a speed of 18 mph for an hour. Jockeys need nerves of steel because the camels can sometimes suddenly stop mid-way through a race without warning!

MAKING A SPLASH

WET AND WILD

Water isn't a person's natural element: our lungs need air, we don't have webbed feet or hands, and we aren't designed for speed in the way that a shark or a seal is. That hasn't stopped us from taking the plunge, though.

Free divers plummet to depths of more than 600 feet using only their finely tuned athlete's bodies. Marathon swimmers race over distances of up to 15 miles in lakes, rivers, or the ocean. Competition divers perform graceful gymnastics before hitting the water at around 34 mph. They're all spectacular.

Taking a dive

Competitive divers perform twists or somersaults in mid-air after jumping from a platform up to 33 feet above the pool. They have just a split second to get everything right. They must enter the water with their body in a vertical position and their arms extended forward—and without making much of a splash.

PROFESSOR SPLASH

From heights of up to 80 feet, Darren Taylor, of Denver, Colorado, dives into tiny, shallow pools, some containing just 12 inches of water! He says the secret is to make a real splash when he lands—that way his fall is cushioned. The impact still leaves his body so bruised that it hurts him to laugh for weeks afterward.

SAY WHAT?

FREESTYLE

In a freestyle race swimmers can use any style—front crawl, butterfly, backstroke, or breaststroke. Most use the front crawl, because it's the fastest.

DIVE IN!

Once a diver has left the board, his or her body must be held in one of four positions.

STRAIGHT: no bend in either the hips or knees

PIKE: knees straight and the body bent at the waist

TUCK: the body is curled up in a tight ball

FREE: a combination of straight, pike or tuck with the legs together

Absolutely nuts

Twiggy the grey squirrel is nuts about water-skiing. Her Florida trainer, Lou Ann Best, taught her to be towed around an inflatable paddling pool by a remote-controlled model boat at speeds of up to 6 mph. Twiggy has demonstrated her skills at boat shows across America.

HIGH DIVE

Tom Daley became the world 10-meter platform diving champion in 2009 at the age of just 15. That made him the youngest diver ever to win a title in men's platform diving. He started diving at age seven and was Britain's youngest competitor at the 2008 Olympics.

It's never too late to start a sport. As a child, Australia's Ian Thorpe was allergic to chlorine (the chemical used in swimming pools), so he didn't swim in his first race until he was seven. Even then the allergy forced him to swim awkwardly with his head out of water.

SLOW STARTER

His nickname was "the Thorpedo" because of his speed in the water.

By age 14 Ian Thorpe was representing his country.

TRIALS OF STRENGTH

FEEL THE FORCE

Some people are so strong they can bend iron bars with their head or pull trains with their teeth. Others can lift cars off the ground, tear thick books with their bare hands, or pull trucks with their hair. For centuries, people have demonstrated their strength by taking part in competitive combat sports such as boxing, sumo wrestling, judo, taekwondo, and karate.

If you don't want to be a real-life muscle man, you could take part in some wackier trials of strength. How about having a go at fish tossing, gumboot hurling, or cell-phone throwing?

It took Rev. Fast 1 minute 16 seconds to pull the plane 29 feet with a rope.

The Globemaster weighed a whopping 207 tons.

The previous record for pulling a plane was 206 tons and it had stood for 12 years.

He trains for his strong-man challenges by pulling his pickup truck up hills.

Strong stomach

Fitness instructor Ken Richmond has such a sturdy stomach he lets people fire cannon balls at it! He can also survive a cannon ball being dropped on his head and withstand the force of a massive 4,000-pound wrecking ball slamming through a concrete wall and into his amazing abdomen.

PLANE CRAZY

In 2009, Reverend Kevin Fast, of Cobourg, Ontario, Canada, managed to pull an enormous military CC-17 Globemaster airplane across the tarmac at Canadian Forces Base Trenton.

FAST MOVER

Ripley explains...

Contact Points used in Karate

- Wrist
- Knifehand
- Back of the hand
- Spearhand
- Ball of the foot
- Instep

In the Japanese martial art of karate, you can punch or kick, but the most famous technique is the knifehand, or karate chop. People can smash over 30 slabs of concrete with just a single karate chop.

Ripley's—— Believe It or Not!

- American martial arts movie star **Bruce Lee** moved his arms and feet with lightning speed. He was so fast he could snatch a dime off a person's open palm and leave a penny behind before they could close their hand.

- To toughen the skin on his fists, he used to regularly thrust his hands into **buckets of rocks and gravel** up to 500 times.

- He could **break wooden boards** that were 6 inches thick with a single punch.

- He could perform **one-handed push-ups** using only his thumb and index finger.

- He could **thrust his fingers** through unopened soda cans.

- He practiced his high kicks by jumping up and tapping people on the ear with his foot.

- He once broke a 150-pound punching bag with a side kick.

EARS!

Zafar Gill, from Pakistan, can lift 121 pounds with one of his ears.

EYES!

Dong Changsheng, from China, pulled a 3,748-pound minibus containing two adult passengers with his eyelids!

Luxembourg's Georges Christen can do just about anything with his teeth. He has towed a 105-ton ship with them, and bent 368 nails with them in an hour. One stunt saw him stop three 110-horsepower Cessna Sport airplanes from taking off at full power—one with his teeth and two with his arms.

TOUGH TEETH

twist it!

In New Zealand, there is an annual contest to see who can throw a gumboot (the heavy rubber boot worn by farmers) the farthest. The winner is presented with a Golden Gumboot!

In Michigan in 1997, Samoan heavyweight boxer Jimmy Thunder knocked out Crawford Grimsley after just 1.7 seconds of their fight.

The first cell phone Throwing World Championships were held in Finland in 2000. One of the sport's top throwers is the UK's Chris Hughff, who can hurl a phone 314 feet. That's a real long distance call!

Ed Byrne from England used his bare hands to karate chop through 55 concrete blocks in less than five seconds... and it didn't even hurt!

STRONG STUFF

ON COURT

More than 46 million Americans play volleyball, and there are around 800 million players worldwide. In fact, soccer is the only sport that more people play across the globe. Like basketball, tennis, squash, and badminton, volleyball is traditionally played on a court. All of these sports require you to be able to run around, have quick reactions, and be very fit. Tennis players can cover 5 miles during a match!

Tennis players can also earn a lot of money. The winners of the singles' titles at Wimbledon in London—the world's oldest tennis tournament—receive $1.3 million. Basketball players can earn even more. Some get paid over $20 million a year!

Michael was so feared that opponents would put two or even three men to cover him every time he touched the ball.

GROWTH SPURT

At high school, Michael Jordan was considered too short to play basketball. Then he grew 4 inches one summer and began the path to superstardom that saw a 1996 sports magazine name him the greatest athlete of the past 50 years. He finished with an incredible career total of 32,292 points, the third highest in league history.

High court

Top tennis players Roger Federer and Andre Agassi needed a head for heights when they played on this court. It was marked out on the helipad of a Dubai hotel 685 feet above ground. If a ball sailed out, nobody went to fetch it!

Lauren Miller's dog Auggie liked to do tricks with tennis balls. He could pick up five in his mouth at the same time!

PLAYING BALL

America's Andy Roddick can serve a tennis ball at 155 mph—that's as fast as an express train.

A game of volleyball that took place in Amstelveen, the Netherlands, in 2008, lasted 60 hours. That's 2½ days!

Basketball-crazy Mike Campbell made 1,338 free throws in an hour—faster than one throw every three seconds—and over 90 percent of his shots were successful.

Twin brothers Ettore and Angelo Rossetti played a continuous tennis rally that lasted nearly 15 hours, with a total of 25,944 shots.

Joseph Odhiambo dribbled a basketball through the streets of Houston, Texas, for 26 hours in 2006.

You have to be really fit to play squash. A squash player can burn up to 1,000 calories during a one-hour game. That's almost twice as many than if you were doing push-ups non-stop for the same amount of time. Phew!

twist it!

IN A SPIN

Using his hands, feet, knees, and even his mouth, American Bruce Crevier can spin up to 21 basketballs at the same time. He has also spun a single basketball on his fingers for over 22 hours. That's nearly a whole day!

SMASHING!

Badminton is played by hitting a shuttlecock made either of goose feathers or plastic. Shuttlecocks can be hit very hard and very fast. A smash by China's Fu Haifeng was recorded at 230 mph.

SISTER ACT

Venus Williams and her younger sister Serena have dominated women's tennis in the 21st century. Between them, they have won over 30 Grand Slam titles.

At the 2007 US Open, Venus served the second-fastest woman's serve ever recorded, 129 mph. The Australian Open tennis speed of beads scattered around the court when a string dreadlocked hair and fell from her tournament her dreadlocked hair and Venus was docked a point at the 1999

SNOW AND ICE

CHILLS AND THRILLS

SNOW TRICKS

Snowboarding is like surfing on snow. Boarders perform lots of tricks. In a U-shaped trench called a halfpipe, they do acrobatic spins and flips and even a trick where they grab their board in mid-air.

If you've ever sped down a hill on a toboggan, you'll know how exciting snow can be. Wherever there is suitable snow and ice, sportspeople can be found competing on it. Speed skiers can hit a breathtaking 150 mph, ski jumpers leap 600 ft while sailing through the air at 65 mph, and teams on bobsleds hurtle around a steep course of solid ice at 90 mph. They all know that the slightest mistake could result in a bad injury.

It's not all about speed. There's the gracefulness of ice skating, the elegance of snowboarding, and the rough and tumble of hockey. So if you thought the best thing about snow was building a snowman, you might have to think again.

DOWNHILL RACERS

Slalom skiers speed down a steep mountain, weaving their way between a series of poles called gates. Nets are placed alongside the course at the most dangerous places, but the skiers still have spectacular falls.

LOONY LUGE

Luge is one of the most dangerous of all sports. Competitors lie down on a fiberglass sled and hurtle feet-first down an icy track at up to 90 mph. They wear little protection, their bodies are just inches from the ice, and the luge has no brakes!

ICE BOWLING

The coolest game of bowling takes place in Japan. Players roll a bowling ball made of ice along a 60-foot lane toward 6¼-inch-high ice pins.

Between 2003 and 2006, American Rainer Hertrich skied for 1,000 days in a row. He once hiked up an active volcano in Chile because it had more snow to ski down than neighboring mountains!

WAYNE'S WORLD

Canadian Wayne Gretzky is the only National Hockey League player to total over 200 points (goals and assists) in a season, and he did it four times. He scored over 100 points in 14 consecutive seasons and was so popular that he used to receive 1,000 fan letters a month.

 At the Montreal Ice Cup, riders race bicycles over a course of sheet ice. They get a grip on the slippery surface by putting up to 400 screws into the rubber tires.

THE WALL

UNUSUAL SPORTS

The World Games is held every four years and features several unusual sports that aren't in the Olympics. These include canoe polo, dragon boat racing, climbing, tug of war, roller hockey, and even dancing. If you prefer your sports a little less energetic, have you ever thought about taking up worm charming or cherry pit spitting? There are many weird and wonderful sports that you can try wherever you live.

PULLING POWER

In tug of war, two teams of eight grip tightly on to either end of a 110-foot-long rope and use their combined strength to pull their opponents over a line. Tug of war was practiced as early as 500 BC by Greek athletes and was an Olympic sport until 1920.

MIGHTY MUSCLES

A Japanese bodybuilder flexes her muscles at the 2009 World Games. Nearly 3,000 athletes from 84 countries took part in the Games.

PIE IN THE SKY

A Canadian and two Australians battle to catch the Frisbee during the flying disk competition at the World Games. The sport can be traced back to the Frisbie Pie Company in Connecticut, where workers played a game in which they threw empty pie tins to one another!

At the World Flounder Tramping Championships in Scotland, people catch fish using their bare feet. They wade into the river and when they feel the flat fish wriggling between their toes, they pick it up. The person who catches the most fish is declared the winner.

If you've got something to shout about, you can do it at the National Hollerin' Contest, held each year at Spivey's Corner, North Carolina. Contestants yell as loud as they can for four minutes—you might want to take ear plugs!

At the Sheep Counting Championships of Australia, several hundred sheep are encouraged to run across a field while competitors try to count them.

twist it!

SPIT THE PIT

Like many established sports, cherry pit spitting started as a casual pastime and has developed into a popular event where people compete at national and international competitions. At the 2006 World Championship in Germany, Franz-Wolfgang Coersten spit a pit an impressive 63 feet 4 inches.

THE EARLY BIRD

The World Worm Charming Championships have taken place since 1980 in Willaston, Cheshire, England. Competitors coax earthworms to the surface by wiggling garden forks in the soil or by pouring water on it. The winner is the person who brings the most worms to the surface in half an hour. In 2009, 10-year-old Sophie Smith won the first prize with a grand total of 567.

MOOOO

POOOO

POLE POSITION

To be crowned pole-sitting champion, you need a head for heights and a lot of patience. In 2002, Daniel Baraniuk won $20,000 after spending 196 days and nights (that's over six months) perched on top of an 8-foot-high pole. His closest rival fell off a month earlier!

COW PATTY BINGO

In some rural areas of North America you can play cow patty bingo. A field is divided into numbered squares, and contestants bet on which square the cow will poop!

TOUCH DOWN

CATCH AND KICK

Each year, football's biggest game, the Super Bowl, is watched on US TV by nearly 100 million people. Football—not to be confused with soccer—grew out of a sport called rugby, which was invented in the UK in the early 19th century. Both football and rugby use an oval-shaped ball. When it hits the ground, its odd shape means that it can bounce in any direction.

To play football or rugby, you need to be strong or fast—better still if you are both. Outside of the USA, football is called American football, but it is played in other parts of the world, too, including Japan, Mexico, and Europe.

Ripley explains...

NFL players have had to wear helmets to protect their heads since the 1940s.

Shoulder pads are made of shock absorbing foam with a hard plastic cover. These protect the players and also make them look much bigger than they really are!

Plastic knee pads fit into pockets inside the football pants. They protect the players' knees when they crash to the ground.

ROUGH AND TUMBLE

Football is fun and fast but also very physical with a lot of body contact. Around 40,000 high-school players suffer concussions (a mild head injury) every year playing football. Quarterbacks or running backs, who are tackled most often, rarely get through a season without being injured.

SCHOOLBOY ERROR

Rugby began in 1823 when William Webb Ellis, a student at Rugby School in England, caught the ball during a game of soccer and ran toward the other team's goal. It is now played in over 100 countries worldwide.

Oooooofff!

GRRRRR

72

<<THE FRIDGE >>

William Perry, a popular defensive lineman for the Chicago Bears, was known as "The Fridge" because of his 6-foot-2-inch, 382-pound square body. Yet at high school he could dunk a basketball!

twist it!

one-yard line.

Footballer Roy Riegels became famous for running the wrong way! Playing for the California Golden Bears in the 1929 Rose Bowl, he picked up a fumble, lost his sense of direction, and ran 70 yards toward his own end zone. He was finally grabbed by one of his team-mates on his own

Jim Purol of California sat in all 92,542 seats at the Pasadena Rose Bowl over a period of five days in 2008. He sat for 12 hours each day and took a cushion to save getting a sore butt.

Willie McQueen was a great defense tackler on the football team at Flint Southwestern Academy High School, Michigan, despite being only 3 feet tall. He had been left with no legs after a railroad accident.

The boys' football team at De La Salle High School, Concord, California, won 151 games in a row from 1992 to 2004.

David Witthoft, a young Green Bay Packers' fan, was so excited by his 2003 Christmas gift—a Packers' jersey with Brett Favre's No. 4—that he wore it every day for over four years.

END ZONE

The French national rugby team have a live cockerel as their mascot. Sometimes he even attends the team's training sessions. It gives them something to crow about!

Rooster booster

PEDAL POWER

Wheels can have up to 48 spokes to help deal with bumpy landings.

Riders can pedal forward and backward for tricks.

BMX magic

BMX (Bicycle Motocross) began in southern California in the 1970s, but is so popular that in 2008 it became an Olympic sport. The bikes are designed for performing tricks and for racing on hilly dirt tracks. Riders must wear a full-face helmet, elbow pads, knee pads, and shin guards. Yet even the best riders sometimes get hurt. American Mat Hoffman has had over 50 surgeries and 500 stitches, and broken almost every bone in his body.

The handlebars can spin in a circle.

There are so many different sports you can do on a bike. Racing cyclists zoom around a track at nearly 50 mph. Cyclo-cross competitors ride through woods and across such rough land that they have to get off and carry their bikes up steep hills. BMX bikers are able to perform fantastic jumps and acrobatic twists in mid-air. In 2008, Kevin Robinson of the USA soared 27 feet into the air on a BMX bike—equal to jumping over a three-story building.

There are endurance races, too. At the Lotoja race in the USA, riders cover 206 miles in a single day. Elsewhere, people ride bikes down glaciers and mountains. They even ride bikes backward—sometimes while playing a musical instrument!

In the Netherlands there are more bicycles (16 million) than there are people.

twist it!

ROUND AND ROUND

Austrian Marcus Stoeckl rode a mountain bike down a snow-covered mountain in Chile, reaching a speed of 130.7 mph.

At the Down the Hill bike race in Taxco, Mexico, competitors ride mountain bikes through a house! They go in through a door, ride down a flight of stairs, and exit through another door.

Jumping from a ramp, Australian Nathan Rennie cleared over 121 ft on his mountain bike in 2005.

At the 2009 X Games in Los Angeles, Anthony Napolitan performed two complete somersaults in mid-air to land the first-ever double front flip on a bicycle.

During the 1904 Tour de France—the world's most famous cycle race—French spectators sprinkled nails and broken glass on the road so that the leaders would get punctures and allow their local favorite to win.

Balancing act

Ripley explains...

When you pedal a bike, you use your muscles to create a force. You are like the engine for your bike. Bicycles are so efficient they can convert 80 percent of the energy you supply at the pedals into energy that powers you along. To compare, a car engine converts only 25 percent of the energy in gasoline into useful power.

It's scary enough riding a bike around volcano craters or on cliff tops, but Canada's Kris Holm does it on a unicycle! The one-wheeled daredevil has ridden on the rail of a 200-foot-high bridge, the edge of a 2,640-foot-high cliff, and within 33 feet of red-hot, bubbling lava on a volcano in Hawaii.

COASTING ALONG

With an oxygen tank on his back, Maaruf Bitar of Lebanon practices his favorite hobby—underwater cycling off the coast of the Mediterranean city of Sidon. Underwater cyclists have ridden at depths of over 200 feet beneath the sea. That's 30 times the depth of an Olympic swimming pool.

23

EXTREME ACTION

Who would think you could play Scrabble underwater or iron a T-shirt at the top of a mountain? You can, thanks to a new range of extreme sports designed to make gentle pursuits or boring jobs much more exciting.

Instead of doing their ironing in the living room, some people do it in caves, in a canoe, on top of a statue, in the middle of a forest, or while snowboarding. It has become so popular that now you can even play Wii extreme ironing—back in your living room!

If only Jim were as eager to iron at home!

Ironing on the roof of a car —Sahara Desert

Extreme housework! Sahara Desert

Don't look down!

Extremely silly

Extreme ironing was thought up by Englishman Phil Shaw in the 1990s and became so popular that the first Extreme Ironing World Championships took place in Germany in 2002. Eighty competitors from ten countries had to think up peculiar places for doing the ironing.

Cliff ironing— not for the faint hearted

Mountain ironing—note the use of crossed skis for an ironing board

BOUNCE

Fred Grzybowski of Los Angeles, California, can jump over a car on a pogo stick. The extreme pogo rider is able to bounce 8 feet into the air and can also perform an incredible nine consecutive pogo backflips. The world championship called Pogopalooza attracts over 60 riders from the USA, Canada, and the UK. The best riders can perform over 220 bounces in a minute.

INSANE IRONING

- Two South Africans ironed while hanging from a rope across a 100-foot-wide mountain gorge.
- A British pair did some ironing at a height of 17,800 feet on Mount Everest.
- In 2007, Henry Cookson dragged his iron and board 1,100 miles across the frozen wastes of Antarctica.
- Australian Robert Fry threw himself off the side of a cliff in the Blue Mountains with an iron, a board, some laundry, and a parachute!
- In 2009, 86 British scuba divers ironed underwater at the same time—in water as cold as 28°F.

EXTREME SCRABBLE

To celebrate the 60th anniversary of Scrabble in 2008, extreme enthusiasts played in some crazy places. Skydivers Nicole Angelides and Ramsey Kent played Scrabble at 13,000 feet above Florida. With each move, they had to glue the tiles to the board to stop them blowing away.

twist it!

ABOVE AND BEYOND

American Peter Jenkins has started a new sport—extreme tree climbing. He and his friends climb trees and perform acrobatic stunts. These include balancing on the branches and running across the canopy (the top) of the trees. They also tree surf, where they go high into the tree on a windy day and ride the branches like waves.

On a 2006 tour, extreme cello players Clare Wallace, Jeremy Dawson, and James Rees carried their musical instruments on to the roofs of 31 different cathedrals in England and played a short concert on each.

In 2008, while orbiting in the International Space Station at 5 miles a second, Canadian astronaut Greg Chamitoff played a game of extreme chess against a team of US students on Earth.

Free running, or parkour, is a form of urban acrobatics. You run through towns and cities, vaulting walls and railings as stylishly as possible, adding spins or twists in mid-air. You can use ledges, handrails, or steps to perform handstands and somersaults. You just make it up as you go along.

SHOW SOME MUSCLE

BODY POWER

Some people can do amazing things with their body. They can squeeze it through the head of a tennis racket—with the strings taken out, of course. They can balance on their head on a high wire barely an inch wide, thousands of feet up in the air without a safety net.

Back on the ground, in 1980 a Japanese man did more than 10,000 push-ups nonstop, and free-running experts can jump between the roofs of buildings, just like in the movies.

IN A SPIN

Kareena Oates from Australia is able to rotate 100 hula hoops around her body at the same time. She has also spun 41 hula hoops around her waist while suspended in the air by her wrists.

UP, UP, UP...

At the Tarragona Castells festival in Spain, acrobats climb over each other to form amazing human towers. There have been as many as ten levels of people standing on each other's shoulders, but sometimes the whole thing just comes crashing down.

Canadian gymnast and acrobat Dominic Lacasse held himself horizontally on a bar as a "Human Flag" for 39 seconds—a display of incredible strength.

ENERGY BUZZ

American Don Claps can perform more than 1,200 consecutive cartwheels, and he can even carry on doing them while drinking water from a paper cup!

In 2009, Davit Fahradyan of Armenia completed 354 arm-aching turns on a horizontal bar.

New Yorker Ashrita Furman hula hooped underwater for 2 minutes 20 seconds at a Florida dolphin center in 2007. He used a special metal hoop and was able to breathe air through scuba-diving equipment.

Olga Berberich did 251 jumps with a rope in just one minute in Germany in 2007.

Los Angeles, California, contortionist Daniel Browning-Smith is so flexible he can squeeze his entire body into a box the size of a microwave oven.

Working in shifts of two people at a time, eight boys, aged between eight and 11, bounced nonstop on an inflatable castle in Michigan for 24 hours in 2008.

twist it!

HUMAN FLAG

GET YOUR SKATES ON

American skater Rob Dyrdek once did 215 ollies in a row.

In 2006, Welshman Dave Cornthwaite spent 90 days on a skateboard, riding it all the way across Australia—a distance of more than 3,500 miles! Skateboarders love to try new challenges. One man jumped over four cars on a skateboard, and another built a skateboard so big that nearly 30 people could stand on it at the same time.

There are now more than 18 million skateboarders in the world. You could also try roller hockey, speed skating, or if you can really stretch your arms and legs, the latest Indian craze of limbo skating!

Dude!

The ollie is one of the most popular aerial skating tricks. You bend down, push your back foot down on the tail end of the board and then allow the board to pop back up. As you leap into the air, the board appears to be stuck to your feet, as if by magic.

GREAT SKATES

Skateboarding was born when Californian surfers wanted something to surf on when the waves in the sea were flat. Believe it or not, top skaters have reached speeds of over 60 mph.

DANNY'S WAY

In Mexico City in 2006, American skater Danny Way landed a sensational backflip, which he called El Camino ("The Way"). He sped down a 75-foot-high ramp and leaped 70 feet through the air at a speed of 50 mph. The previous year he had jumped over the Great Wall of China on a skateboard. Not bad for someone who says he is afraid of heights!

Roller skates first became popular in the 1880s.

The lowdown

Limbo skaters have to be strong and flexible to skate under more than 50 parked cars at a time. They practice for months to get their body into the right position. Young limbo skater Aniket Chindak can roller-skate under parked cars that are just 9½ inches off the ground.

twist it!

TURNING HEADS

At the 1999 X Games, American Tony Hawk became the first skater to land a 900: that's 2½ rotations in mid-air.

Bingo, a Border collie, used to ride through the streets of Winnipeg, Canada, on a skateboard, picking up litter.

In 2000, Richie Carrasco completed 142 dizzying 360-degree spins on a skateboard without stopping.

A roller skate invented by a Frenchman, M. Mercier, in the 1900s was powered by a two-cylinder gasoline engine, enabling the skater to zoom along at 19 mph.

Around 280 roller skaters held on to the waist of the person in front of them to form a giant skating chain that snaked through the streets of Singapore City in 2006.

Rohan Ajit Kokane is so good at limbo skating he can do it under cars while blindfolded!

SPEED SKATER

Ripley's Believe It or Not!

ROLLER MAN

Frenchman Jean-Yves Blondeau wears a special plastic suit with sets of rollers attached. It means he can roll down the highway at up to 60 mph. He can even overtake motorbikes!

29

GOAL CRAZY

SENSATIONAL SOCCER

About 3.5 billion people either play or watch soccer, making it the world's most popular sport. Every country plays the game, right down to tiny islands. On the Isles of Scilly, off the southwest coast of England, the league is made up of just two teams who play each other every week! It does mean the draw for the cup is not very exciting...

Soccer is fast and skillful. Some people love the game so much they name their children after their favorite players, dye their hair in their team's colors, or travel thousands of miles just to watch their team. The best players are treated like superstars and are paid over $150,000 a week. Boys and girls play soccer, but you need to be fit to be a professional, as some top players run up to 6½ miles during a match.

GOAL CRAZY

Freezing Footie

Jungfrau Mountain — Switzerland

International soccer players staged a 2007 exhibition match on an artificial field laid out on a glacier. It took place in the shadow of Switzerland's 13,642-foot Jungfrau Mountain. The high-altitude air was so tiring that the teams played just five minutes each half.

L CRAZY

Dan Magness
Britain

Using his feet, thighs, chest, and head, Britain's Dan Magness kept a soccer ball in the air for 24 hours. He touched the ball around 250,000 times, knowing that the smallest lapse in concentration would mean he would have to start all over again!

FREE KICKS

Some soccer matches are decided by penalty shoot-outs, where eight kicks are often enough to get a result. At the end of a 2005 Namibian Cup tie in Africa, the penalty contest went on for an incredible 48 kicks and lasted nearly an hour!

Important soccer matches often attract crowds of over 70,000 people, but the 1950 World Cup final between Brazil and Uruguay was watched by nearly 200,000 spectators.

An annual soccer match called the Calcio takes place in Florence, Italy, between two teams of 27 players dressed in 16th-century costume. It is a rough game, and players are allowed to elbow, kick, and even head butt each other!

Welsh soccer fan Steve Thatcher named his son after all the players in his favorite team, Cardiff City. It means young Sam has 12 middle names!

twist it!

GOAL CRAZY

GOOOAAALLL!!!
Nani — Portugal

Portuguese soccer star Nani performs his famous backflip celebration after scoring a goal for English team Manchester United. The fans love it— as long as he doesn't injure himself doing it.

GOAL CRAZY

Tiny Field — Microscopic

Created by technology, this soccer field is so tiny that 20,000 of them could fit on the tip of a single human hair. It has all the markings of a full-sized field but can only be viewed using a really powerful microscope.

GOAL CRAZY

The Legendary Pelé
Pelé — Brazil

The great Brazilian soccer player Pelé scored 1,281 goals in his career—more than any other professional player. He helped his country to win the World Cup three times, and scored the opening goal in the 1970 final when Brazil beat Italy 4–1.

GOAL CRAZY

Brainy Ball
Adidas — Germany

Adidas has designed a clever soccer ball. It contains a chip that sends a radio signal to the referee's watch in less than a second of the ball crossing the goal line. So there should be no more arguments about whether or not a shot was a goal.

GOAL CRAZY

On the Head
Manoj Mishra — India

Indian soccer fan Manoj Mishra won a competition by balancing a ball on his head for 14 hours. He practiced yoga exercises so that he could get used to keeping still for so long. Afterward, he dedicated his success to his hero, Argentinian soccer legend Diego Maradona.

HIGH

TAKING TO THE SKIES

Many humans love to fly. As we don't have wings like a bird, we try the next best thing and take up sports such as hang gliding, paragliding, ballooning, gliding, and skydiving. American skydiver Don Kellner has made over 36,000 jumps, and Jay Stokes once made 640 jumps in a single day! **Skydivers free fall at 120 mph before the safety parachute opens and they descend gently to the ground.**

If you are worried about heights, you don't have to go up alone. You could always take your dog with you. Brutus, a miniature dachshund from California, made more than 70 jumps with his owner!

Mike Howard, an airline pilot, walked along a 19-foot-long pole from one balloon to another. When he had blindfolded in 2004. When he walked from Bristol, England, the daring tightrope walk, parachuted to the ground.

YEEE-HAAAA...

WAA-HOOOO...

JUMP!

Skydivers jump from airplanes, helicopters, and even hot-air balloons. Once their parachutes are open, they control their direction by pulling toggles on the end of steering lines attached to the chute. That's how they can land on a small cross marked on the ground after jumping from 13,000 feet.

Believe It or Not!®

Buddy the Labrador and his owner, Bill Kimball of San Diego, California, went hang gliding together for more than eight years. Buddy joined Bill on over 75 flights.

twist it!

In Japan they stage kite fights. Competing teams tie sharp razor blades and broken glass to the tail strings of their kites and fly them against one another. The aim is to rip the opposing kite to shreds so that it can no longer fly.

In just eight days, Englishman Martin Downs skydived on six continents: Africa, Europe, South America, North America, Australia, and Asia.

Vijaypat Singhania flew a hot-air balloon to an incredible altitude of 68,986 feet over India in 2005.

In 2004, Bob Holloway flew 2,580 miles in a powered paraglider from Astoria, Oregon, to Washington, Missouri.

SUPERFLY GUYS

Holly Budge from England skydived over Mount Everest in 2008. She jumped from a plane at 29,500 feet and on her descent reached speeds of 140 mph and braved temperatures of −40°F.

Ripley explains...

Sail

Rigging

Harness

Control Bar

Hang gliders can stay thousands of feet in the air for hours, soaring through the skies like an eagle. A hang glider has a lightweight aluminum frame, a big nylon wing, and no engine. The pilot is attached to the frame by a harness. There are no switches or buttons to worry about. Pilots steer by shifting their body weight on the frame; then all they have to do is relax and admire the views.

<<human bird>>

American Jeb Corliss comes as close as any human has to flying. Wearing a special winged jumpsuit, he takes part in the scary sport of proximity wingsuit flying. He jumps from a helicopter or off a cliff edge thousands of feet up and flies terrifyingly close to mountain faces. Jeb flew down the 14,692-foot-high Matterhorn mountain in Switzerland within 5 feet of the jagged cliff-face, reaching speeds of 100 mph.

SURF'S UP

RIDING THE WAVES

It's not only waves that are a danger to surfers. Each year, as many as 80 surfers are attacked by sharks.

84 surfers rode the same wave at the same time off the coast of Brazil in 2007.

Have you ever wished you could ride a wave on a surfboard? Some waves are huge—up to 70 feet high. That's more than four times the height of an adult giraffe! That just makes it even more of a challenge for a surfer. You can surf a wave standing up, crouching, or lying down—and some surfers have managed to stay on the same wave for half an hour. There are no rules, you just do what you enjoy.

The first surfers—in Tahiti in the 18th century—used planks of wood, but today's surfboards are made of lightweight polyurethane foam. Surfing is really popular in places like California, Florida, and Hawaii, where the shape of the seabed and strong winds create big waves.

RIDING HIGH

Kite surfers use wind power to help them speed across the water and soar up to 162 feet in the air. They stand on a board and hold on to a large controllable kite. The aim is to do tricks such as jumps, spins, and even somersaults, and to see how high and long they can jump off waves.

SAY WHAT?

CATCH A WAVE

This is when you launch yourself into the path of a suitable wave.

Kite surfers can go great distances when the wind is behind them. In 2006, UK kite surfer Kirsty Jones traveled 140 miles from Lanzarote, in the Canary Islands, to Morocco.

PLAIN SAILING

Windsurfers attach a sail to their surfboards. When the wind blows into the sail from behind, it makes the board go faster: sometimes up to 60 mph! Windsurfers can perform amazing stunts, jumps, and spins.

Donald "D.J." Dettloff has created a colorful fence from more than 700 surfboards near his home in Hawaii.

Ripley's Believe It or Not!®

In California, they have a surfing contest that's just for dogs. Four-legged surfing dudes show their style on their own and with human partners. The winner receives a basket full of dog treats.

35

IN THE RUNNING

MARATHONS

People can't run as fast as cheetahs, but they can run for longer distances. They need great stamina to do this. The longest running race in the Olympics is the marathon at just over 26 miles.

Just running a marathon is really exhausting, but some athletes need greater challenges. So they run extreme—or ultra—marathons that are a whopping 100 miles long. Occasionally, someone will even run all the way around the world—with lots of stops, of course!

The first marathon

In 490 BCE, Pheidippides, a Greek soldier, ran about 25 miles from the town of Marathon to Athens to announce that the Greeks had defeated the invading Persians in battle. The route was exhausting, and shortly after arriving in Athens Pheidippides fell to the ground dead.

In 1896, the first modern Olympic Games in Athens held a race of roughly the same length in his honor. It became known as the marathon.

MARATHON FACT FILE

- More than **400,000 people** in the USA compete in marathons annually.
- More than **800 marathons** are run in the world each year. The biggest marathons can have tens of thousands of runners.
- A marathon runner will go through **two pairs of sneakers** while training for the race.
- Top marathon athletes will run **100 miles** a week in training.
- It takes the average woman **51,214 steps** to complete a marathon.
- In 2008, 64-year-old Texan Larry Macon ran **105 marathons**.

Sand marathon

A competitor climbs a sand dune during the 2009 Marathon des Sables in the Sahara Desert. This desert marathon is considered the hardest in the world.

COOL RUNNING

Runners tackle rough mountain trails in the 2006 Everest Marathon. The starting line is at 17,000 feet near Mount Everest Base Camp in Nepal, making it the highest marathon in the world.

HAVING A BALL

There are many ways to complete a marathon. This man at the 2008 Berlin Marathon was running in a sphere!

<< Bringing up the rear

Englishman Lloyd Scott walked the 2002 New York and London marathons wearing a 120-pound antique diving suit. In London, it took him five days and eight hours. In 2003, he wore the same suit to complete a marathon underwater!

STAYING POWER

Dave Heeley from England ran seven marathons on seven continents in seven days in 2008, even though he is blind.

Michal Kapral, from Toronto, Canada, ran a marathon in 3 hours 7 minutes in 2005 while juggling three balls at the same time.

Between 1997 and 2003, England's Robert Garside ran 30,000 miles around the world in 2,062 days.

US soldier Jake Truex ran 5,000 meters in just over 22 minutes in Germany in 2006 with a heavy 40-pound backpack strapped to his back.

Charlie Engle (USA), Ray Zahab (Canada), and Kevin Lin (Taiwan) ran the same distance as two marathons a day for 111 days to cross the 4,000-mile Sahara Desert on foot in 2007. They had to cope with temperatures that were over 100°F by day, but below freezing at night.

DID YOU KNOW?

¡¡ 1ST...¡¡

At the London Marathon...

They use 710,000 bottles of water, 950 portable toilets, 500 stretchers, and 68 ambulances.

The blue paint that marks out the course is steam-cleaned off as the last runner passes, so the streets of London can be quickly returned to normal.

Australia's Kurt Fearnley completed the 2009 race in a wheelchair in a record 1 hour 28 minutes 56 seconds.

The London Marathon was the first to be run over 26.2 miles. This is because at the 1908 Olympics the Royal Box lay 385 yards beyond the 26-mile finish line. The race was extended so that it could finish beneath the Royal Box.

RISKY BUSINESS

Cave divers plunge to depths of up to 100 feet underwater in total darkness at the risk of losing their way or running out of air. Kayakers ride over the world's highest waterfalls, hitting terrifying speeds of 70 mph on the way down. Bungee jumpers leap from bridges high above raging rivers with one end of an elastic cord tied to their ankles and the other end tied to the jumping-off point. For some people, sport is only fun if they are putting their life at risk.

Over the past 30 years, dozens of dangerous sports have been introduced that are exciting to do but, when things go wrong, can result in serious injury, even death. Only really physically fit people should attempt these sports—and even then they must have the right equipment, or the consequences could be fatal.

In the balance

This is not a trick photo. Eskil Ronningsbakken really is performing a one-handed handstand while balancing on the edge of a ladder attached to a 1,000-foot-high cliff in Norway. He was able to do it by adding 330 pounds of weights at the balancing end. It still looks pretty scary though.

SAY WHAT?

BASE JUMPING

BASE jumping is named after the places you jump from: Buildings (skyscrapers, statues), Antennas (radio masts, cranes), Spans (bridges), and Earth (cliffs).

DEATH DEFYING

Have you ever wondered what it is like to be a hamster in a wheel? Well, the sport of Zorbing lets you find out. Zorbanauts roll down hills inside large transparent plastic spheres, reaching speeds of over 30 mph.

CRAZY KAYAKING

One of the world's top extreme kayakers is fearless Jesse Combs from Oregon. Jesse risks life and limb by taking his kayak over steep crashing waterfalls, such as this 70-foot drop at the Mesa Falls in Idaho.

A NEED FOR SPEED

David Kirke, founder of England's Dangerous Sports Club, adapted a medieval rock-throwing device called a trebuchet so that humans could be catapulted 55 feet into the air in under two seconds.

Bull running takes place in several Spanish towns, most famously in Pamplona. Participants have to run in front of a herd of angry bulls that have been let loose in the streets. Fifteen people have been killed in the Pamplona event since 1910.

Tyler Bradt paddled a kayak down the raging waters of the 107-foot Alexandra Falls in Canada, and didn't flip once.

In 1991, John Kockelman made a bungee jump of 1,000 feet from a hot-air balloon 5,000 feet above California.

In BASE jumping, people hurl themselves from tall structures with just a parachute to save them from certain death. The thrill is to wait as long as possible before pulling the parachute cord. Here, Leaping 915 feet from the Menara Kuala Lumpur Tower in Malaysia, this jumper will have six seconds of freefall before he has to use his parachute.

People have **BASE jumped** from San Francisco's Golden Gate Bridge, the Eiffel Tower in Paris, and New York City's Empire State Building.

In 2006, Australians Glenn Singleman and Heather Swan jumped off a **21,500-foot-high** precipice on Meru Peak, India, and managed to land on a 16,500-foot-high glacier.

In 2006, Dan Schilling made **201 BASE jumps** in 24 hours off a bridge 46 feet above the Snake River Canyon, Idaho. He kept jumping even after fracturing his wrist.

An average of **15 people** are killed BASE jumping every year.

TWIST it!

HAVING A BALL

Believe it or not, golf was the first sport to be played on the Moon. Astronaut Alan Shepard hit a couple of shots on the 1971 *Apollo 14* Moon mission. Ball games such as golf, bowling, pool, and table tennis are played all over the world. Baseball also has a wide following, and an amazing 42 million people play it in the USA alone. Cricket is played in the UK, Australia, and India, but hardly at all in America.

Most of these sports are over 100 years old, and some have their origins in ancient history. A form of bowling was played in Egypt as far back as 3200 BCE. The game was outlawed in England in 1366 because King Edward III wanted his soldiers to concentrate on archery practice instead.

The odds of a spectator being hit by a ball at a Major League game are 300,000 to 1.

Nearly 80 million people pay to watch Major League baseball in a season.

Big teams like the New York Yankees average attendances of over 50,000 per game.

The athletic **Nomar Garciaparra** first played for the Boston Red Sox in the 1990s. He is one of only a handful of players in Major League baseball history to have hit two grand slams (a home run hit when there are runners at three bases) during a single game.

UPSCALE BALL

Instead of being covered in leather, this cricket ball is covered in 2,704 diamonds. Made in Sri Lanka, it is said to be the first life-sized diamond-and-gold cricket ball in the world.

twist it!

The following text appears upside-down:

English golfer Andrew Winfield teed off from the summit of Africa's Mount Kilimanjaro in 2008, 19,340 feet above sea level.

Playing baseball for Portsmouth High School, Ohio, in 2008, triplets Howard, John, and Matt Harcha all hit home runs, in the order of their birth from oldest to youngest.

In 2007, English golfer David Huggins hit his third hole-in-one... and he was only eight years old.

Table tennis was first played in Victorian England in the 1880s on a dining room table, often using a cigar box lid as a bat, a champagne cork as a ball, and a row of books as a net!

Every Thanksgiving, Cincinnati, Ohio, hosts a Turkey Bowl, where competitors bowl frozen turkeys instead of bowling balls!

PLAY BALL

CRICKET ODDITIES

- Cricket is played by two teams of 11 players. One team bowls (pitches) and fields while the other bats. A team is in (at bat) until ten of its batsmen are out. Then the other team is in!

- Batsmen try to score runs by hitting the ball a long way. If a batsman is out for no runs, he has scored a duck— because zero is shaped like a duck's egg.

- The bowlers aim at three wooden stumps in the ground known as the wicket. They take it in turn to bowl "overs," which consist of bowling six balls at the batsman. If no runs are scored off an over, it is called a maiden.

- There are ten ways a batsman can be out, including bowled, caught, and leg before wicket (lbw).

BILLION-DOLLAR MAN

American golfer Tiger Woods became the first ever athlete to earn a billion dollars. He has won more than 70 tour events and when he was only three years old he shot an amazing score of 48 over nine holes at a golf club in California. He usually wears a red shirt on the final round of tournaments because he believes it helps him to win.

Perfect pitch

Jim Abbott was a Major League baseball pitcher in the 1990s even though he was born with only one hand. In 1993, playing for the New York Yankees, he even pitched a no-hitter (where the opposing team has no hits in an entire game) against the Cleveland Indians. This was a fantastic achievement because on average just two no-hitters a year have been thrown in Major League baseball since 1875.

WACKY RACES

FUN RUNS

You don't need an engine to take part in a wacky race, just a daft sense of humor. In various places across the world people push, pull, or carry beds, outhouses, coffins, even their wives—all in the name of sport.

For serious athletes who like a fun run, there is the mad dash up the stairs of the Empire State Building. Germany's Thomas Dold won in 2006, 2007, 2008, and 2009, and he also excels at another crazy form of racing—running backward!

BIRDS IN FLIGHT

Lightweight jockeys ride ostriches in a race in Shanghai, China. Ostrich racing is also popular in South Africa and in several locations in the USA. Ostriches can run at 45 mph, the fastest running speed of any bird. Ostriches are harder to steer than horses, so although the jockeys have special saddles and reins, they still regularly fall off.

STEP UP THE PACE

Each year over 300 runners take part in a race up the stairs of the Empire State Building. The climb to the observation deck is up 1,050 feet, 86 floors, and 1,576 stairs. It takes most of the runners about 15 minutes to reach the observation deck. The building's elevator can get there in less than a minute.

NYRR Empire State Building
RUN-UP

DEAD FUNNY

Every year in Manitou Springs, Colorado, teams race coffins with a living female occupant. Around 40 coffins take part. They are rerunning the legend of Emma Crawford, who died in 1890 and was buried on top of Red Mountain, only to have her coffin slide down the canyon in 1929 after heavy rains.

Quackers!

More than 200,000 blue plastic ducks floated half a mile downstream on the River Thames near London for the 2009 Great British Duck Race. Each duck had a number and people picked a duck, hoping that theirs would be the first to reach the finish and win them a cash prize.

IN IT TO WIN IT

People race decorated outhouses through the streets of Dawson City in Canada! For the Great Klondike Outhouse Race, teams speed around a 1½-mile course. One person has to sit on the toilet the whole time!

In Sydney, Australia, there is a race solely for women wearing high stiletto-heeled shoes. The trick is to get to the finish line without spraining your ankle.

There's a Grand Prix in France that's just for homemade pedal cars. Drivers pump their legs around Valentigney for up to three hours, but design is just as important as speed. That's why you might see a man in a monkey mask driving a banana-shaped car!

How about doing the 100 meters... on stilts? In the Philippines, competitors perch on top of 6-foot stilts made of bamboo and walk along the course as fast as they can.

Marry and carry

Estonia's Madis Uusorg carries his wife Inga Klausen to victory in the 2007 Wife-carrying World Championships in Finland. The race is run over an obstacle course and the winner receives his wife's weight in beer.

FUN AND GAMES

OLYMPIC DREAMS

The Olympic Games are the greatest sporting show on earth. The ancient Olympics were held in Greece starting in the 8th century BCE—nearly 3,000 years ago. Sports included the javelin, long jump, running in armor, and even kissing! After a long break, the Olympics were brought back in 1896 and are now held every four years. An incredible 4.5 billion people watched the 2008 Olympics in Beijing, China, either on TV or online.

In Beijing, more than 11,000 athletes from around 200 countries competed in more than 300 events, from athletics to wrestling. The Winter Olympics are just as exciting, featuring sports such as skiing, ice skating, and bobsled. The winner of each event receives a gold medal, second place gets a silver medal, and third place gets a bronze medal. These are the most important prizes in sport.

STEVE REDGRAVE

A powerful rower, Britain's Steve Redgrave (second from left) in 2000 was one of only four Olympians to have won a gold medal at five consecutive Olympic Games.

Fan-tastic

To celebrate the 2008 Olympics in Beijing, a Chinese man, Dr. Wei Sheng, pierced his head, face, hands, and chest with 2,008 needles in the five colors of the Olympic rings.

EDWIN MOSES

4,200 athletes from 148 countries took part in the 2008 Paralympics. These games are for athletes with a physical disability or vision impairment. Sports include wheelchair basketball and wheelchair tennis.

Edwin Moses of the USA won gold in the 400 meters hurdles at both the 1976 and 1984 Olympics. Between 1977 and 1987 he was undefeated, winning a record 122 consecutive races.

US swimmer Michael Phelps won eight gold medals at the 2008 Beijing Olympics. It was the first time that this had been achieved by a competitor at a single Olympic Games.

Live pigeon shooting was an event at the 1900 Olympics. Nearly 300 birds were killed. It was the first and only time in Olympic history that animals were killed on purpose.

GOING FOR GOLD

At the 1904 Olympics, George Eyser (USA) won six gymnastics medals, including three gold, despite having a wooden left leg.

Women were not allowed to compete in track and field events at the Olympics until 1928. However, so many collapsed at the end of the 800 meters in that year that the event was banned until 1960.

A 1956 Olympic water-polo match between Hungary and the USSR (modern-day Russia) was abandoned after the teams started fighting underwater.

After winning a rowing gold medal at the 1956 Olympics, 18-year-old Russian Vyacheslav Ivanov quickly lost it. He threw the medal into the air in celebration, but it landed in the lake. He dived in but was unable to find it.

The USA are the reigning Olympic rugby champions. That's because rugby was last featured in the Olympics in 1924 when the USA beat France 17–3 in the final.

Party time

The opening ceremony at the 2008 Beijing Olympics featured over 15,000 performers and a spectacular display of 35,000 fireworks. The four-hour ceremony cost $100 million—that's nearly $7,000 per second— making it the most expensive in the history of the Olympics.

CLARA HUGHES

Canada's Clara Hughes is one of only a few athletes to win medals at both the Summer and Winter Olympics. She succeeded at both cycling and speed skating.

MICHAEL PHELPS

INDEX

Bold numbers refer to main entries; numbers in *italic* refer to the illustrations

A

Abbott, Jim 41, *41*
abdomen, cannon balls fired at 12, *12*
acrobats 26, 27
Adidas 31, *31*
Adoye, Ajibola 44
Agassi, Andre 14, *14*
airplanes 6, 12, *12*, 13
Angelides, Nicole 25, *25*
Antarctica, extreme ironing in 25
athletes **44–45**
Auer, Dirk 29, *29*

B

backpack, running marathon with 37
badminton 14, 15, *15*
balancing, on cliff edge 38, *38*
ball games **14–15**, **40–41**
balloons, hot-air 32, 33, 39
balls
  balancing on head for 14 hours 31, *31*
  diamond-covered cricket ball 40, *40*
  football 20
  juggling while running marathon 37
  keeping in air for 24 hours 30, *30*
  signals to referee 31, *31*
  spinning basketballs 15, *15*
  tennis 14, *14*, 15, *15*
Baraniuk, Daniel 19
BASE jumping *38*, **38–39**
baseball 40, *40*, 41, *41*
basketball 14, *14*, 15, *15*, 44
Beijing Olympics 7, 44–45, *45*
Berberich, Olga 27
Best, Lou Ann 11
bicycles 17, **22–23**
Bifar, Maaruf 23, *23*
bingo, cow patty 19, *19*
blind man, runs multiple marathons 37
blindfolded
  limbo-skating under cars 29
  tightrope walking between balloons 32
Blondeau, Jean-Yves 29, *29*
BMX bikes 22, *22*
boats
  dragon boat racing 18
  pulling with teeth 13
  rowing 44, *44–45*, 45
  speedboats 6
bobsleds 16, 17, *17*, 44
body piercing, multiple 44, *44*
bodybuilding 18
Bolt, Usain 6, 7, *7*

boot-throwing contest 13
bouncy castles 27
bowling 17, *17*, 40, 41
boxing 13
Bradt, Tyler 39
bridges, BASE jumping from 39
Browning-Smith, Daniel 27
Budge, Holly 33
bull running 39
bungee jumping 38, 39
Byrne, Ed 13

C

camel racing 8, 9, *9*
Campbell, Mike 15
cannon balls, fired at stomach 12, *12*
canoe polo 18
Carrasco, Richie 29
cars
  energy efficiency 23
  extreme ironing on 24
  jumping over on pogo stick 25, *25*
  pedal car racing 43
  roller-skating under 29, *29*
  speed **6–7**
cartwheels, multiple 27
catapulting humans 39
cathedrals, playing cellos on roofs of 25
cave diving 38
cell phone throwing championships 13
cellos, extreme playing 25
Chamitoff, Greg 25
chariot racing 8
cheetah races 9
cherry pit spitting 19, *19*
chess, playing in space 25
Chindak, Aniket 29, *29*
Christen, Georges 13, *13*
Claps, Don 27
cliffs
  balancing on edge of 38, *38*
  BASE jumping from 39
  extreme ironing on 24, 25
climbing 18, 25
cockerel mascot 21
Coersten, Franz-Wolfgang 19, *19*
coffin races 42, *42*
Combs, Jesse 39, *39*
concrete, karate chops 13
concussion 20
contortionists 27
Cookson, Henry 25
Corliss, Jeb 33, *33*
Cornthwaite, Dave 28
courts, ball sports **14–15**
cow patty bingo 19, *19*
Crawford, Emma 42
Crevier, Bruce 15, *15*

cricket 40, 41
cyclocross 22

D

Daley, Tom 11, *11*
dancing 18
Dawson, Jeremy 25
deserts
  extreme housework in 24
  running marathons in 36, 37
Dettloff, Donald "D.J." 35, *35*
diamond-covered cricket ball 40, *40*
disabled athletes 44
diving 10–11, *10–11*, 25, 38
dogs
  hang-gliding 33, *33*
  picking up tennis balls 15, *15*
  races 9
  skateboarding 29
  skydiving 32
  surfing 35, *35*
Dold, Thomas 42
Downs, Martin 33
dragon boat racing 18
duck races 43, *43*
Dyrdek, Bob 28

E

elephant polo 9, *9*
Ellis, William Webb 21
Empire State Building, New York City 39, 42, *42*
endurance races, cycling 22
energy, bicycles 23, *23*
Engle, Charlie 37
Everest, Mount
  extreme ironing on 25
  running marathon on 37, *37*
  skydiving over 33
extreme sports **24–25**
Eyser, George 45

F

Fahradyan, Davit 27
Fast, Reverend Kevin 12, *12*
Favre, Brett 21
Fearnley, Kurt 37
Federer, Roger 14, *14*
fence, made of surfboards 35, *35*
fighting, with kites 33
fireworks, Beijing Olympics 45, *45*
fish, catching with bare feet 19
flag, human 27, *27*
flying **32–33**
football **20–21**
Formula 1 racing 6, 7
Foyt, AJ 6
free running 26, *26*
freestyle swimming 10
frisbies 18, *18*
frog races 9

Fry, Robert 25
Fu Haifeng 15
Furman, Ashrita 27

G

Garciaparra, Nomar 40
Garside, Robert 37
glacier, soccer match on 30, *30*
gliders 32
golf 40, 41, *41*
Greece, ancient 8, 18, 36, 44
Gretzky, Wayne 17, *17*
Grimsley, Crawford 13
Grzybowski, Fred 25, *25*
gumboot throwing contest 13
gymnastics 45

H

hang-gliding 32, 33, *33*
Hawk, Tony 29
Heeley, Dave 37
helipad, playing tennis on 14, *14*
helmets, football players 20, *20*
Hertrich, Rainer 17, *17*
hills, rolling down in plastic spheres 39, *39*
hockey
  ice hockey 16, 17, *17*
  roller hockey 18
Hoffman, Mat 22
hollerin' contest 19
Holloway, Bob 33
Holm, Kris 23, *23*
horse races 8
hot-air balloons 32, 33, 39
house, cycling through 23
housework, extreme 24
Howard, Mike 32
Huggins, David 41
Hughes, Clara 45, *45*
Hughff, Chris 13
hula hoops 27, *27*
Humphreys, Alastair 23
hurdling 44, *44*

I

ice, racing bicycles on 17
ice bowling 17, *17*
ice hockey 16, 17, *17*
ice skating 16, 44, 45, *45*
inline skating 29, *29*
International Space Station 25
ironing, extreme **24–25**

J

Jenkins, Peter 25
Jimmy Thunder 13
jockeys 8, 9, 42, *42–43*
Jones, Kirsty 35
Jordan, Michael 14, *14–15*
juggling, while running marathon 37
Jungfrau Mountain 30, *30*

K

Kapral, Michal 37
karate 13, *13*
kayaking, over waterfalls 38,
 39, *39*
Kellner, Ron 32
Kent, Ramsey 25, *25*
Kilimanjaro, Mount, playing
 golf on 41
Kimball, Bill 33, *33*
Kirke, David 39
kite fighting 33
kite surfers 35, *35*
Kockelman, John 39
Kokane, Rohan Ajit 29

L

Lacasse, Dominic 27, *27*
lawn mower, motorized 7
Lee, Bruce 13, *13*
legless football player 21
limbo-skating 29, *29*
Lin, Kevin 37
London Marathon 37
luge 17, *17*

M

Macon, Larry 36
McQueen, Willie 21
Magness, Dan 30, *30*
Maradona, Diego 31
marathons **36–37**
martial arts 13
Mears, Rick 6
medal, lost in lake 45
Mercier, M. 29
Miller, Lauren 15
Mingay, Matt 7
Mishra, Manoj 31, *31*
moon, playing golf on 40
Moses, Edwin 44, *44*
motorcycles, speed 6, *6*, 7
Mouch, C.G. 7
mountains
 BASE jumping from 39
 cycling down 23
 extreme ironing on 24, *24*
 playing golf on 41
 running marathons on 37
 soccer match on 30, *30*
muscle power **26–27**
music 22, 25

N

nails, bending with teeth 13,
 13
names, boy named after
 soccer players 31
Nani 31, *31*
nanotechnology, soccer field
 31, *31*
Napolitan, Anthony 23
Netherlands, bicycles 23

O

Oates, Kareena 27
Odhiambo, Joseph 15

Olympic Games 7, 8, 9, 18,
 36, 37, **44–45**
ostrich racing 42, *42–43*
outhouses, racing 43
overalls, fire-proof 7

P

Palio, Siena 8, *8*
Pamplona, bull running 39
parachutes 32, 38, *38–39*
paragliding 32, 33
Paralympics 44
parkour 26, *26*
Pasadena Rose Bowl 21
pedal car racing 43
Pelé 31, *31*
penalty shoot-outs, soccer 30
Perry, William 21
Pheidippides 36
Phelps, Michael 44
phone throwing championships
 13
pigeon shooting 45
pigs 9, *9*
plastic duck races 43, *43*
pogo stick, jumping over car
 on 25, *25*
pole sitting 19
polo
 canoe polo 18
 on elephants 9, *9*
pool 40
Purol, Jim 21
push-ups 13, 15, 26

R

racing **6–9**
Redgrave, Steve 44, *44*
Rees, James 25
Rennie, Nathan 23
Richmond, Ken 12, *12*
Riegels, Roy 21
Robinson, Kevin 22
Roddick, Andy 15
roller hockey 18
roller-skating 29, *29*
Ronningsbakken, Eskil 38, *38*
Rossetti, Ettore and Angelo
 15
rowing 44, *44–45*, 45
rugby 20, 21, 45
running 6, 7
 backwards 42
 free running 26
 hurdling 44
 marathons **36–37**
 one-armed runner 44
 stiletto heel races 43
 up stairs 42

S

Sahara Desert, marathons in
 36, 37
Schilling, Dan 39
Scott, Lloyd 37, *37*
Scrabble, extreme 24, 25, *25*
shark attacks, surfers 34

Shaw, Phil 24
shed, motorized 7
sheep-counting championship
 19
Shepard, Alan 40
Shields, George 7
shoes, stiletto heel races 43
shooting pigeons 45
shouting contest 19
shuttlecocks 15, *15*
Siena, Palio 8, *8*
Singhania, Vijaypat 33
Singleman, Glenn 39
skateboarding **28–29**
skating
 ice skating 16, 44, 45, *45*
 inline skating 29, *29*
 limbo-skating 29, *29*
 roller-skating 29
ski jumping 16
skiing 16, *16–17*, 44
skydiving 32
 dog 32
 multiple jumps 32
 over Mount Everest 33
 on six continents 33
 playing Scrabble 25, *25*
skyscrapers,
 BASE jumping 38, *38–39*
 playing tennis on top of 14,
 14
slalom skiing 16, *16*
sleds 17, *17*
Smith, Sophie 19
snow **16–17**
snowboarding 16, *16*
soccer 14, 21, **30–31**
somersaults, on bicycle 23
space, playing chess in 25
spectators, at soccer match
 31
speed **6–9**
sphere, running marathon in
 37, *37*
spitting cherry pits 19, *19*
squash 14, 15
squirrel, water-skiing 11, *11*
stairs, running up 42, *42*
stiletto heel races 43
stilt-walking races 43
Stoeckl, Marcus 23
Stokes, Jay 32
stomach, cannon balls fired at
 12, *12*
strength **12–13**
Super Bowl 20
surfing **34–35**
 tree surfing 25
Swan, Heather 39
swimming **10–11**, 44

T

table tennis 40, 41
Taylor, Darren 10, *10*
teeth, strength 13, *13*
tennis 14, *14*, 15, *15*, **44**
Thatcher, Steve 30

Thorpe, Ian 11, *11*
throwing contests 13
tightrope walking, between
 balloons 32
toboggans 16
toilets, outhouse racing 43
Tour de France 23
towers, human 27, *27*
trebuchet 39
trees, extreme climbing 25
triplets, play baseball 41
Truex, Jake 37
tug of war 18, *18*
turkeys, bowling frozen 41

U

underwater
 cave diving 38
 cycling 23, *23*
 extreme ironing 24, 25
 hula hoops 27
 playing Scrabble 24
unicycles 23, 23
Unser, Al 6
Uusorg, Madis 43, *43*

V

volcanoes
 riding unicycles on 23, *23*
 skiing down 17
volleyball 14, 15

W

wacky races **42–43**
Wallace, Clare 25
water polo 45
water-skiing squirrel 11, *11*
waterfalls, kayaking over 38,
 39, *39*
waves, surfing **34**
Way, Danny 28, *28–29*
Wei Sheng, Dr. 44, *44*
wheelchair sports 37, **44**
wife-carrying championships
 43, *43*
Williams, Venus and
 Serena 15, *15*
Wimbledon tennis
 championships 14
windsurfing 35, *35*
Winfield, Andrew 41
wingsuit, flying in 33, *33*
Winter Olympics 44, 45
Witthoft, David 21
Woods, Tiger 41, *41*
World Games **18**
worm charming 18, 19
wrestling, with pigs 9

X

X Games 23, 29

Z

Zahab, Ray 37
Zorbing 39, *39*

ACKNOWLEDGMENTS

COVER (t/l) © Speedfighter – Fotolia.com, (c) © Diego Cervo – Fotolia.com, (c/l) © Feng Yu – Fotolia.com, (t) © Albo – Fotolia.com, (b/r) www.jw-sportfoto.de; **2** (b) Reuters/Claro Cortes, (t) Anja Niedringhaus/AP/Press Association Images; **3** Georges Christen; **4** (b/l) © Michael Lawlor – Fotolia.com, (b/c) © kamphi – Fotolia.com, (t) iStock.com, (b/r) © Terry Morris – Fotolia.com; **5** (t/r) © Thomas Lammeyer – iStock.com, (b/l) © Michael Lawlor – Fotolia.com, (b/cl, b/c, b/cr) N & B – Fotolia.com, (b/r) Pawel Nowik – Fotolia.com, (r) © Feng Yu – Fotolia.com; **6** (b/l) Reuters/United Photos; **6–7** (dp) Reuters/Stringer USA; **7** (r) Anja Niedringhaus/AP/Press Association Images; **8** Reuters/Stefano Rellandini; **9** (t/l) Reuters/Fahad Shadeed, (b/r) Reuters/Claro Cortes, (b) Reuters/Chaiwat Subprasom; **10** (l) Phil Walter/Getty Images, (t/r, c) Michael Martin/Barcroft Media Ltd, (b/r) © Chepko Danil – iStock.com; **11** (r) John Chapple/Rex Features, (t/l) Tony Gentile/Reuters, (b/r) Reuters Photographer/Reuters; **12** William Tremblay wl_tremblay@ hotmail.com; **13** (t/l) Archive Photos/Getty Images, (b/r) Georges Christen; **14** (b/r) Mike Hewitt/Getty Images; **14–15** (t) Nathaniel S. Butler/NBAE/Getty Images; **15** (b/l) © Thomas Lammeyer – iStock.com, (b/r) Toby Melville/Reuters, (c) David E. Klutho/Sports Illustrated/ Getty Images; **16** (t) © Pierre Jacques/Hemis/Corbis, (b) Gary Caskey/Reuters; **17** (t/r) Reuters/Yuriko Nakao, (t/l) © Reuters/Corbis, (r) S Levy/Getty Images; **18** (l) Sam Yeh/AFP/Getty Images, (t/l) Reuters Photographer/Reuters; **18–19** Sam Yeh/AFP/Getty Images; **19** (t/l) Heribert Proepper/AP/Press Association Images, (b/r) © Julien Rousset – Fotolia.com; **20** (l) David Purdy/Landov/Press Association Images, (r) © George Peters – iStock.com; **20–21** (dp) © Peter Baxter – Fotolia.com; **21** (t/l) Lynne Cameron/PA Wire/Press Association Images, (l) Jonathan Daniel/Getty Images, (b/r) Damien Meyer/AFP/Getty Images; **22** Lester Lefkowitz/Corbis; **23** (l) seanwhite.net/Sean White Photography, (r) AFP/Getty Images; **24** (t/l, t/r, c, b, r) Rex Features; **25** (t/l) Barcroft Media via Getty Images, (t/r) Barcroft Media Ltd; **26** (t) © Maxym Boner – iStock.com, (l) © Arturo Limon – iStock.com, (b/r) © Bart Sadowski – iStock. com; **27** (l) Alfaqui/Barcroft Media Ltd, (t/r) Samantha Sin/AFP/Getty Images, (r) Ermann J. Knippertz/AP/Press Association Images; **28–29** (c) Doug Pensinger/Getty Images, (b) Anthony Acosta; **29** (b/l) www.jw-sportfoto.de, (b/r) ChinaFotoPress/Cheng Jiang/ Photocome/Press Association Images, (t/r) © Simon de Trey-White/Barcroft Pacific; **30** (t/l) Reuters/Christian Hartmann, (c) Johnny Green/PA Wire/Press Association Images; **30–31** (dp) Stephen Pond/Empics Sport; **31** (t/l) Wenn, (t) Kin Cheung/AP/Press Association Images, (t/r) © Reuters/Corbis, (b/r) © EuroPics [CEN], (b/l) Rex Features; **32** © Daniel Ramsbott/epa/Corbis; **33** (b/l, b) © Axel Koester/ Corbis, (t/l) Sam Barcroft/Rex Features, (r) © Daniel Cardiff – iStock.com; **34** Neale Haynes/Rex Features; **35** (l) Warren Bolster, (r) © Don Bayley – iStock.com, (b/l) Denis Poroy/AP/Press Association Images, (b/r) John Hugg: mauisurfboard.com; huggsmaui.com; **36** Pierre Verdy/Getty Images; **37** (l) Getty Images, (t) Reuters/Str New, (c) Reuters/Pawel Kopczynski; **38** (sp) Sindre Lundvold/Barcroft Media, (b/r) Sipa Press/Rex Features; **39** (l) Photograph by Darin Quoid, (t/r) © Jörg Hackemann – Fotolia.com; **40** (sp) Paul Spinelli/ MLB Photos via Getty Images, (b/r) Sena Vidanagama/Stringer/Getty Images; **41** (t/r) iStock.com, (b/l) John Zich/AFP/Getty Images, (b/r) Dave Martin/AP/Press Association Images; **42** (b/l) Reuters/Brendan Mcdermid, (b/r) Andra DuRee Martin; **42–43** (t) Reuters/Nir Elias; **43** (l) Reuters/Lehtikuva Lehtikuva, (t/r) Jonathan Hordle/Rex Features, (t) © Michael Flippo – iStock.com; **44** ((b/l) Sipa Press /Rex Features, (c) ChinaFotoPress/Photocome/Press Association Images; **44–45** (dp) © Luc Santerre Castonguay – iStock.com, (t/r) Bob Jones/Rex Features; **45** (b) Reuters/Staff Photographer, (l) Rex Features, (b/r) Reuters/Max Rossi

Key: t = top, b = bottom, c = center, l = left, r = right, sp = single page, dp = double page, bgd = background

All other photos are from Ripley's Entertainment Inc. All artwork by Rocket Design (East Anglia) Ltd.

Every attempt has been made to acknowledge correctly and contact copyright holders and we apologize in advance for any unintentional errors or omissions, which will be corrected in future editions.